PEOPLE WHO HELP US

FARMER

Rebecca Hunter

Photography by Chris Fairclough

CHERRYTREE BOOKS

A Cherrytree book

First published in 2008 by
Evans Brothers Ltd
2A Portman Mansions
Chiltern Street
London W1U 6NR

British Library Cataloguing in Publication Data
Hunter, Rebecca,
    Farmer. - (People who help us)
    1. Farmers - Juvenile literature 2. Agriculture - Juvenile
    literature
    I. Title
    630

ISBN-13: 9781842345139

Planned and produced by Discovery Books Ltd
Editor: Rebecca Hunter
Designer: Ian Winton

Acknowledgements
Commissioned photography by Chris Fairclough.

The author, packager and publisher would like to thank Peter and Fiona Bridge, Edward Bridge, Trish Bridge
and David Bridge for their participation in this book.

Words appearing in bold, **like this**, are explained in the glossary.

Contents

I am a farmer

My name is Peter.
I am a farmer.

I have an **organic dairy farm** in Shropshire.

Several men work on the farm with me.
My family also helps out quite a lot. This
is my son Edward, my sister Trish and my
wife Fi outside the stables with our horses.

It is 5 o'clock in the morning.
I have to get up early to get
the cows in for milking.

We milk the
cows twice a day.
They know when it is time for
milking and come in quite willingly.

6

Most of my cows are Montbeliarde cows. They are red and white and come from France.

The cows wait in the yard behind the **milking parlour**.

The milking parlour

The cows file into the parlour. They each have a stall to stand in.

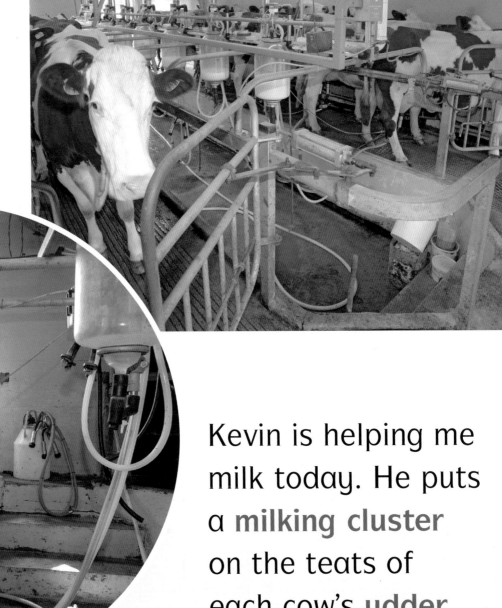

Kevin is helping me milk today. He puts a **milking cluster** on the teats of each cow's **udder**.

We collect the milk in jars. Each cow produces about 20 litres of milk a day.

When we have finished milking a cow, each teat is dipped in **iodine solution**.

The iodine cleans the teat and stops any **infection** starting.

Cleaning up

After milking there is a lot of cleaning up to do. I wash the outside of the bulk tank. The milk is stored and cooled in the bulk tank.

Then I hose down the yard. The cows have gone back to the fields.

The milk lorry arrives to take the milk away. The milk will go to the dairy. Here it is **pasteurized** and bottled. Then it is sent to the shops.

It is 9 o'clock and I am hungry. I go back to the house and have a big breakfast with Fi.

Feeding calves

Now it is time to feed the calves. Fi gives them some of the milk saved from the milking.

This calf was only born yesterday. She can't drink from a trough yet so Fi feeds her from a bottle.

Trish gives the calves some calf pellets.

These calves are a bit older.
I give them some straw to eat.

Making silage

Today we are making **silage**. Silage is made from cut grass. The cows eat it during the winter when the grass stops growing.

The grass was cut yesterday.
This tractor is turning it to dry it out.

I use a big tractor
with a trailer
to pick up
the grass.

When the trailer is full, I swap it for an empty one.
Another tractor takes the full one back to the farm.

Silaging is hard work. I am very glad to see Fi arriving with my lunch!

It is nice to get down off the tractor for a few minutes, but I can't stop for long. We have to collect all the grass before it rains.

Back at the farm a tractor
pushes the cut grass into
a pile called a clamp.

Selling a bull

A local farmer needs a new bull. He has come to look at some of my bulls.

He likes one of them and wants to buy it. We agree on a price and shake hands.

I go to the farm office and find the bull's **passport**. I enter the details of the new owner on the computer.

19

Slurry Spreading

Out in the fields one of the men is spreading **slurry**. Slurry is liquid **manure**. It is used to **fertilize** the fields.

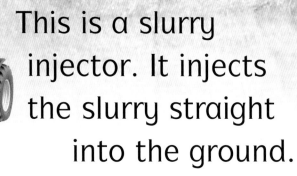

This is a slurry injector. It injects the slurry straight into the ground. It does not make a mess of the field like a normal muck-spreader. Cows can **graze** on the grass right after spreading.

Edward and I go down to the silage clamp. The men have covered the cut grass with plastic and weighed it down with old tyres. It is important to keep all the air out. Edward and I put the last few tyres in place.

In a few months the grass will have turned into silage. The cows will enjoy it over the winter.

Evening milking

It is now 4 o'clock. It has been a busy day on the farm, but it is not over yet. Edward and I set off to get the cows in for evening milking.

If you like working with animals and being outdoors, being a farmer is a great life.

Glossary

dairy farm a farm that keeps cows to produce milk

fertilize to put things on the land to make grass and crops grow better. Manure is a type of fertilizer.

graze to eat grass

infection an illness caused by germs

iodine solution a liquid that kills germs

manure animal waste

milking cluster the equipment that pumps the milk out of a cow's udder

milking parlour the building in which cows are milked

organic using only natural products with no chemical fertilizers or pesticides

passport a document that shows who a person or animal is

pasteurize to heat milk to a very high temperature to kill bacteria and germs

silage cut grass that is sealed and stored and used as food for cows

slurry liquid animal waste

udder the part of a cow that produces milk. Young calves drink milk from the cow's udder.

Index